WOOL GATHERING

Wool Gathering

Sheep Raising
in Old New England

by ELIZABETH GEMMING

*Illustrated
with prints and photographs*

Coward, McCann & Geoghegan / New York

PICTURE CREDITS: pages 2, 8, 9, 13, 25 left, 26, 29, Old Sturbridge Village photos by Donald F. Eaton; 5, 24 left, 24 right, 25 right, also Old Sturbridge Village; 6, 17, 32, 45, Klaus Gemming; 7, 14, 23, 31, 38 (Merino sheep), also 19, *An American Dictionary of the English Language*, 1864; 10, 40 (wood engravings by John Warner Barber, ca. 1840), The Society for the Preservation of New England Antiquities; 15, Western Regional Research Center, U.S. Dept. of Agriculture, Albany, Calif.; 16, American Wool Council, Denver; 22, Plimoth Plantation, Plymouth, Mass.; 30 (coverlet, detail), National Gallery of Art, Index of American Design, Washington; 35, Eleutherian Mills-Hagley Foundation, Wilmington, Del.; 39 (*Old Grist Mill* by George H. Durrie, 1853), Wadsworth Atheneum, Hartford, The Ella Gallup Sumner and Mary Catlin Sumner Collection; 42 (weathervane, gilded copper), The Eleanor and Mabel Van Alstyne Folk Art Collection, Smithsonian Institution Photo No. P65, 254; 43 (*Village Post Office* by Thomas Waterman Wood), New York State Historical Association, Cooperstown.

Copyright © 1979 by Elizabeth Gemming

All rights reserved. This book, or parts thereof, may not be reproduced in any form without permission in writing from the publishers.
Published simultaneously in Canada by Longman Canada Limited, Toronto.

Library of Congress Cataloging in Publication Data
Gemming, Elizabeth. Wool gathering.

   Includes index
   SUMMARY: Describes sheep-raising and the wool industry in colonial New England. Includes a discussion of the production of woolen yarn and cloth.

   1. Sheep—New England—History—Juvenile literature. 2. Wool trade and industry—New England—History—Juvenile literature. 3. Woolen and worsted manufacture—New England—History—Juvenile literature. 4. Wool—Juvenile literature. [1. Sheep—New England—History. 2. Wool trade and industry—History. 3. Wool] I. Title.
SF375.4.N33G45   338.1'7'6300974   78-24378
ISBN 0-698-20482-4

PRINTED IN THE UNITED STATES OF AMERICA

CONTENTS

1   Shearing Time   7
2   What Is Wool?   14
3   Custom-Tailored   23
4   The Amazing Merino   31
5   Westward Ho!   38
    How to Make a Muffler   46
    Index   47

1 Shearing Time

 At last, at last, winter is past—it will soon be summer! The birds are singing in the leafy green trees, and pink roses and wild flowers are blooming everywhere. If you were a boy or girl in rural New England a hundred or a hundred and fifty years ago, you would be looking forward to sheep shearing.

In early America, shearing time was the most exciting festival of the farmer's year. It was much more than just another yearly chore. It was a merry time when people gathered to watch the shearers compete. The contestants used hand clippers just like our garden shears, and their goal was to clip off each fleece all in one piece and as fast as possible.

A popular nineteenth-century writer, Rowland Robinson, born in the heart of the Vermont sheep-raising country, remembered how the spectators cheered, and how "shearers, many of whom were often the flock-owners' well-to-do neighbors, were treated more as guests than as laborers, and the best the house afforded was set before them."

And what a festival it was! Ordinary chores and cares were put aside, Robinson reported, and "the great barns' empty bays and scaffolds resounded with the busy click of incessant shears, the jokes, songs, and laughter of the merry shearers, the bleating of the ewes and lambs, and the twitter of disturbed sparrows, while the sunlight, shot through crack and knot-hole, swung slowly around the dusty interior in sheets and bars of gold that dialed the hours from morning to evening."

Shearing was done after "lambing" but before "turning-out time"—after the birth of the spring lambs but before the flock was put out to pasture for the summer. This was generally in late May or early June, whenever the sheep could survive without the warm fleeces that had grown deep and thick during the rugged northern winter. (Mild weather was a must, for sheep catch cold easily and even a chill rain can make them sick.)

Of course, not every shearing was a party. Small families or people in isolated settlements managed to get the sheep shorn without much fuss. One Connecticut boy, in the early 1800s,

took care of the shearing with his uncle. The two simply filled up a gallon jug with cider (for refreshments) and hiked down to the river outlet to wash the family sheep. The boy recorded the event in his journal: "We built an inclosure of rails and drove the sheep in. The old ram we boys used to drag in and souse under. He would come out and stand dripping." One day later, they sheared the grumpy old ram and the other sheep and, as the boy confessed, "The only difficulty with me was, I used to cut in and take out a little piece of the skin now and then."

Sheep thrived on the salt meadows near the ocean, and of all the shearings in New England, the most famous was held

annually on Nantucket Island, Massachusetts, off the coast of Cape Cod. The town of Nantucket was a picturesque settlement around a fine natural harbor. It was known as the "Little Gray Lady by the Sea" because it was a town of weatherbeaten, gray-shingled houses inhabited by gray-clad Quakers, some of them wealthy and most of them engaged in hunting the whale on three- or four-year voyages to the vast Pacific.

Nantucket sheep lived all year round on the flat, boggy moors that made up the center of the windswept, almost treeless island. A very thin layer of vegetation—mostly bayberry and heather—rooted in sand and gravel and peat, provided food for the flocks on the commons. The commons were the unfenced, open lands that lay between villages and between individually owned farmsteads—in the earliest days, the moors had been owned in common, that is, by all. Later, the commons were divided into shares, with each shareholder receiving the right to graze a fixed number of sheep on common pasture.

Sheep on the Nantucket moors endured a hard life, without sheepfold or shepherd. In winter storms, they often strayed to the dunes and to the edge of the bluffs above the slate-gray sea and the foaming surf. Occasionally, the howling wind would tumble one or another over the brink to its death on the beach below, and sometimes sheep were buried under snowdrifts. But most of them survived, their heavy fleeces encrusted with frozen salt spray, by grubbing under the snow for bits of plants to eat and by huddling close together for warmth.

Eventually, a few better-sheltered pastures were set aside on the outskirts of several villages. A few gates had to be put up across dirt roads to keep the "town flock" from trampling kitchen gardens during the night.

For years, the entire population of Nantucket and their guests celebrated shearing, camping out overnight for the two-day festival. Nantucket shearing was held (as the Quakers put it) "on the Second and Third Day nearest the 20th of Sixth Month"—on the Monday and Tuesday nearest the twentieth of June.

Shearing served as a kind of family reunion, a homecoming time for friends and relatives who had moved away. People came by boat, as the Nantucketers phrased it, "on from off"—to the island from the mainland.

Tents and booths were set up on the shores of the freshwater ponds where the sheep were to be washed before being clipped.

With its chain of ponds, Miacomet Plain, on the west side of the island, was a favorite spot, and to this day one of the ponds is still known as Washing Pond.

By daybreak on Shearing Monday, lines of two-wheeled "tip-carts" had already begun to creak along the deeply rutted sandy tracks toward Miacomet. Four-wheeled box-wagons followed, equipped with built-in seats or with one seat and two kitchen chairs set up in back. Passengers settled in the rear, drivers stood in front, and they all lurched and bounced and clung to the ends of ropes to keep from being dumped out.

Near the ponds, sails were stretched on poles to provide shade for the shearers. On the grass adjoining the washing ponds, people also spread out sails in which to wrap the freshly shorn fleeces. All day long, from booths nearby, poor widows and unmarried women sold cookies, cakes, and preserves for pennies. (Unmarried women were called "spinsters" because so many of them earned their modest living spinning thread and yarn.)

For most islanders, shearing was the next best thing to a circus. An old book written by a visiting off-islander describes the excitement this way:

"Seldom did a sheep escape his shearer's hands without one or more patches of tar [nicks and scabs] to show where scissors had gone deeper than the fleece. The next thing was to rebrand each animal with its owner's initial or emblem; and then the shearing was over, and the encampment broke up, the lads and lasses finishing out the holiday with a surreptitious dance in town—for these were the days of Quaker supremacy, when dancing, music, cards, and most modes of amusement were strictly forbidden."

During the coming summer, thousands of fleeces would be "carded"—combed to remove tangles and burs—and then spun into yarn from which new winter clothes would be made. The flax plants had hardly been harvested from home gardens and painstakingly processed into linen thread and cloth before the whole cloth-making process began all over again with wool. Many a young girl was tempted to embroider her sampler with the old familiar motto:

Flax in winter, wool in summer; woman's work is never done.

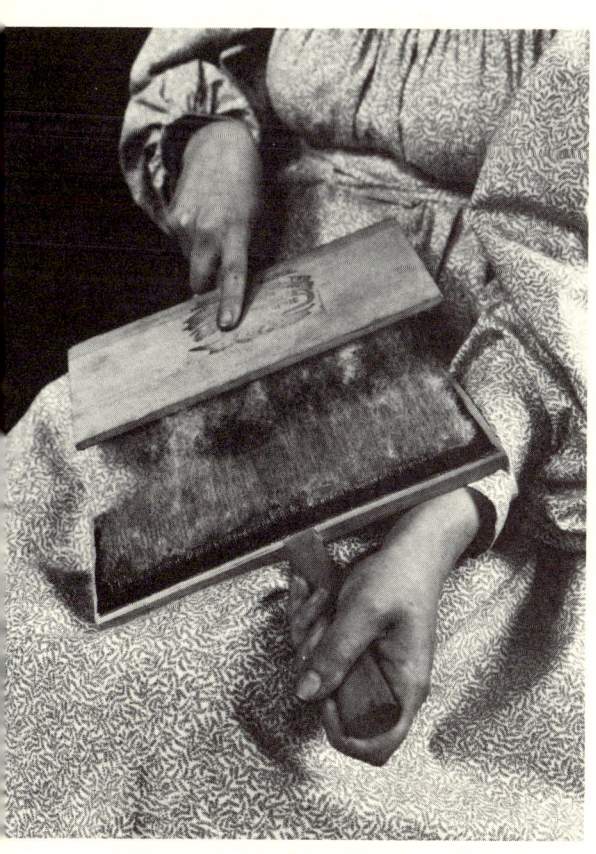

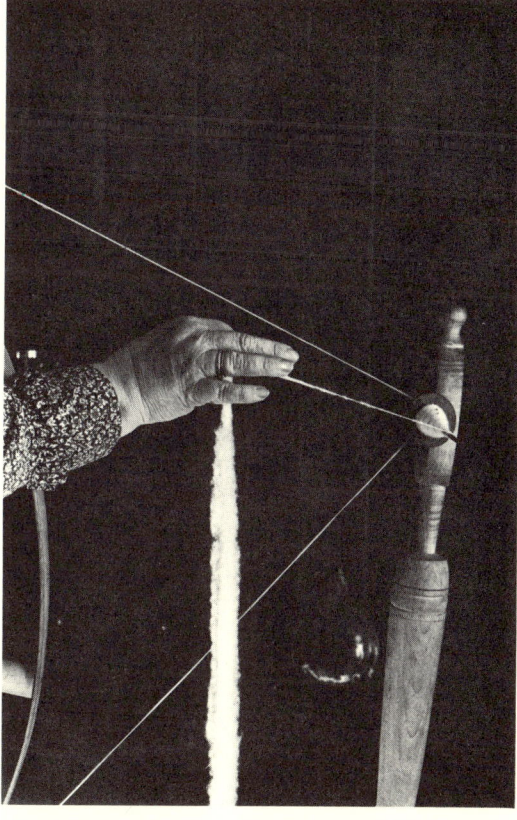

2 What is Wool?

Wool covers the bodies of certain mammals. All mammals have some kind of protective hair or furlike covering, but not all bear wool. "Wool" means the natural fibers that make up the fleece or coat of such an animal—for example, the *domestic* sheep. (Another domestic animal that bears wool is the alpaca, a South American relative of the camel.)

Many mammals have two types of fibers in their coats: the primary fibers, an outer coat of coarse "guard hairs"; and the secondaries, more numerous, fine, short fur hairs that trap an insulating layer of air next to the animal's skin. *Wild* sheep have both types of fibers: an outer coat of hair and an undercoat of wool (which is much softer).

Wool fibers are solid. They are solid "cylinders" made up of a protein called keratin, with a scaly surface that permits the fibers to be compressed together to form felt, a non-woven fabric.

Hairs are made of keratin too, but they are hollow. Guard hairs, except at base and tip, are actually "tubes" of keratin that have a central air space, broken up by thin partitions. (Our fingernails and toenails are also made of keratin.)

Like hair, a wool fiber consists of two parts: the "root," which is under the surface of the mammal's skin and is alive; and the "shaft," which is above the surface of the skin and is

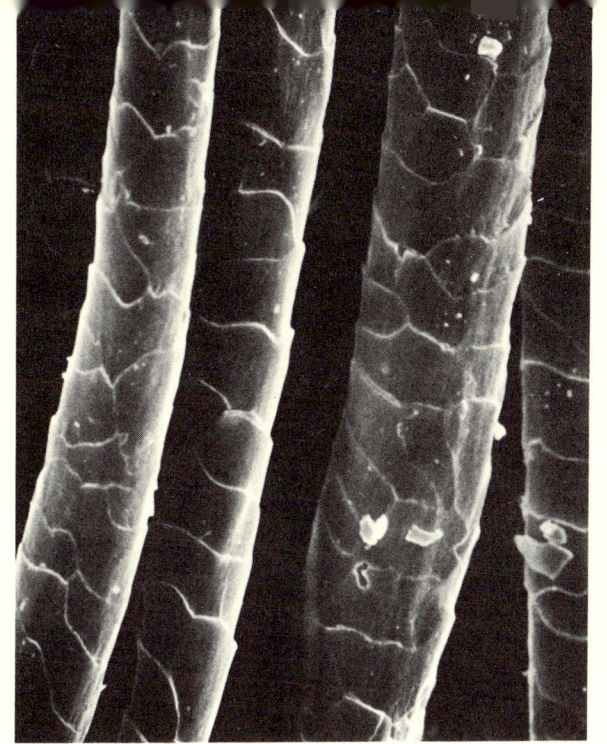 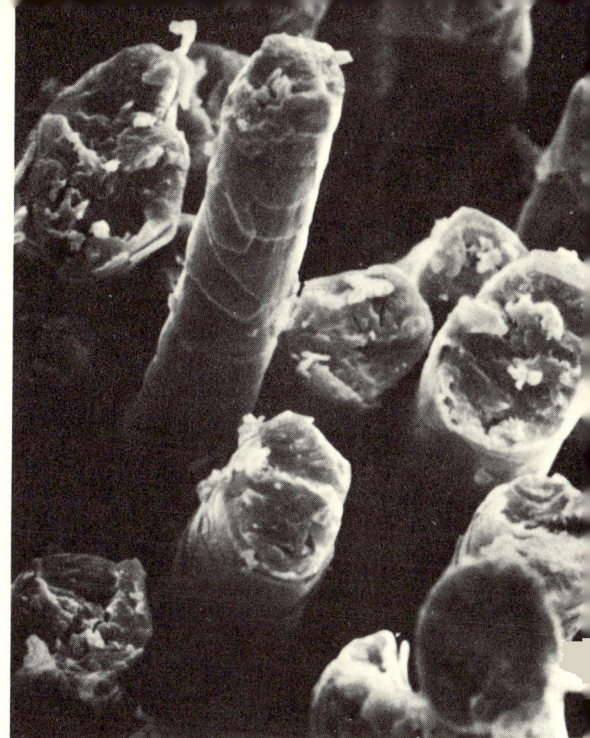

dead. Both wool and hair grow from "follicles," tiny tubelike holes in the inner layer of the skin. In general, hair grows relatively straight and wool grows with a crimp, or wave, that gives it elasticity—so that wool bounces back like a spring after it is stretched and let go. The shaft of a wool fiber consists of overlapping cells in two layers—millions of irregular scales like roof shingles but too tiny to be seen under an ordinary microscope.

New hairs grow as old hairs are shed. Normally, a hair root does not grow continuously. Follicles on the human scalp and those of most wool-bearing sheep have something in common: They have unusually long growth periods—several years at a time—and brief resting periods. Other mammals moult, or shed, regularly with the changing seasons. Wild sheep generally shed their soft undercoat in summer, and early people learned

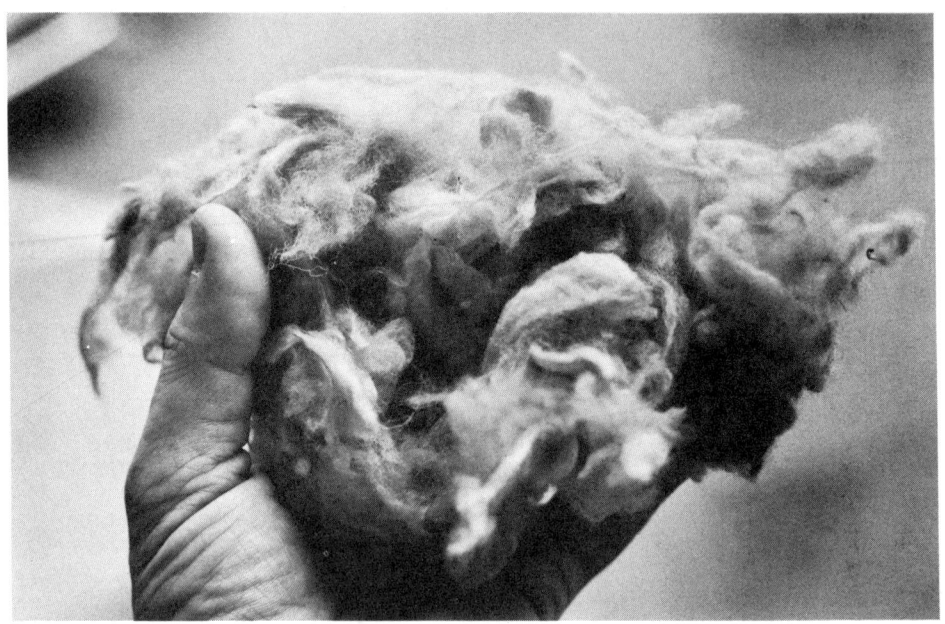

to pluck this wool in late spring. (This primitive method of gathering wool by hand was called "rueing.")

Wool is nature's own "miracle fiber," and no laboratory-invented fiber has managed to improve on or even match wool's special properties. Wool is strong, and its unique springiness makes it last a long time. When wool fabric is rubbed or stretched, the tension is distributed over all the fibers.

The crimp in wool fibers enables the fabric to trap air as insulation. So wool keeps us warm, and it also keeps us cool! For thousands of years, nomads in the deserts of North Africa and the Near East have worn flowing woolen robes and head coverings that keep them comfortable in the searing heat of day as well as in the bitter cold of night. And since wool does not conduct heat, wool garments do not feel clammy even when wet.

Wool does not soil easily, but it can take dye and hold color beautifully. During the dyeing process, color is absorbed by the fiber itself, and is not merely a surface coating. So wool resists fading. Wool is flame-resistant, and if it does catch fire, it tends to burn slowly, gives off no harmful fumes, and often extinguishes itself. It will not drip or melt the way some synthetic fibers do.

A sheep always wears a natural raincoat, for wool is water-repellent. Wool fabric sheds water, for the membrane that surrounds the wool fibers is like a coating of wax. At the same time, tiny pores do admit moisture, very gradually, into the fiber's absorbent inner cells, which helps in the long run to make the fabric wrinkle-resistant.

Natural wool is usually some shade of white, although sheep also can bear fleeces of tan, gray, brown, or black. The length

and the fineness of the fibers found in various breeds of sheep determine how different kinds of wool will be used. A sheep's fleece is generally finest over the animal's shoulders and coarsest on its legs.

Through careful breeding over thousands of years, the coarse outer *hair* of the wild sheep has been gradually displaced by a soft undercoat of *wool*. Some modern domestic sheep have hair only on face and legs; all the rest of their coat is wool. Today, the breeds of sheep are classified worldwide according to the characteristics of their fleeces:

1. *Fine-wool.* Most of these breeds are descendants or variants of the Spanish Merino sheep, which has a small body in proportion to the weight of its fleece. Their wool is very thick, short, and fine.
2. *Long-wool.* These are quite large sheep, with heavy, coarse fleeces. They are bred for meat as well, particularly in England and Australia.
3. *Crossbred-wool.* A typical modern wool-and-meat sheep.
4. *Medium-wool.* A farm sheep, raised in small flocks, primarily for meat.
5. *Coarse-wool.* A typical example is the wiry-haired karakul, a wild sheep of Central Asia.

Wild sheep were originally found only in the Northern Hemisphere, over a wide arc of mountains and high plains. Wild sheep, in fact, are still most at home in the highest, rockiest, most remote regions, where food is very scanty. (Wild sheep of modern times include the moufflon of Europe and the bighorn sheep of the North American Rocky Mountains.)

Moufflon

Rocky Mountain Sheep

The sheep was almost certainly the first wild animal to be domesticated by human beings, probably at least eight thousand years ago, in central Asia. By nature, sheep are rather timid and display a strong flocking instinct. Long ago, people must have noticed that sheep were easy to handle and tended to "follow the leader." Even before they settled down as farmers, the hunters and food gatherers of prehistoric times had become shepherds.

Sheep can graze just about anywhere and can digest the coarsest of grasses. If it had not been for sheep, millions of acres of grassland on every continent on earth would have, through the ages, proved uninhabitable by human beings.

Sheep provide meat and also milk, which can be drunk right away or stored for future use in the form of cheese. Sheep supply leather for boots and slippers, pouches and saddlebags, even tents.

The nomadic herdsmen of the plains of central Asia were able to migrate, with the changing seasons, to colder or warmer or drier or wetter climates—and to higher or lower altitudes—because their flocks of sheep were a walking supply of food and fiber. People learned to adapt their wardrobes and convert their portable dwellings. They insulated themselves against heat, cold, wind, and rain with sheep's wool and sheepskins.

Early people did not clip the wool from their sheep—they simply picked off loose clumps of fleece and gathered up fibers shed by sheep as they grazed. Working first with their fingers, people may have attempted to intertwine wool fibers in lasting and pleasing ways. Some people devised tools of wood or bone to help in their work—the remains of simple spindles have been discovered in ancient graves in the Near East. Then someone tried stringing strands of wool fiber up and down on a frame of wood, and interlacing other strands crosswise, inventing the first woven cloth. It may be that the earliest textiles were not woven on a loom but knitted or crocheted—interlooped with a single strand of yarn by means of the fingers or one or two sticks or bones used as knitting needles or crochet hooks. Whichever process was invented first, both crafts are very, very old.

Ancient writings prove that as early as 4000 B.C., the Babylonians were wearing woolen clothing. (The name Babylon actually means "Land of Wool.") The making of cloth may have originated there.

Wool was one of the first goods to be traded among nations. Travelers shared ideas and customs as they bargained in the marketplaces and bazaars of Africa and the Near East.

Domestic sheep came to Europe by way of Greece, a barren and rugged land where poets sang of sheep and shepherds. The poets of ancient Rome also sang of sheepherding and the pastoral way of life, and the ancient Hebrews, too, were devoted shepherds on stony heights and in parched semideserts.

The Romans, extending their mighty empire, took sheep to North Africa and Western Europe. Roman soldiers are believed to have established England's first real woolen factory, about 50 A.D., at Winchester. From this small beginning, England went on to become the world's leading producer of wool and woolen cloth, and remained so for hundreds of years.

Spain, which also was part of the Roman Empire, had ideal weather and terrain for the raising of sheep. The climate is harsh and dry, and much of the land is rough and barren of plant life other than scrawny grasses. There, early in the first century A.D., the Romans undertook the first scientific breeding of sheep. They created the Merino, which is one of the world's great "foundation breeds" and has the finest fleece of all. The Moors, Arabs from North Africa who conquered Spain in the eighth century, fostered the breed and carried on a busy wool trade throughout the Mediterranean world during the early Middle Ages.

In much of Europe, the Middle Ages were a time of turbulence, upheaval, and hard times. Yet monks managed to keep alive the ancient craft of weaving with wool in spite of wars, famine, and poverty. Spain and England eventually emerged as arch-rivals in the world wool trade during the great age of trade and exploration.

The first sheep to reach the East Coast of North America probably came in Dutch ships, in the early 1600s. The Dutch

pastured small flocks on Manhattan Island. The Plymouth Pilgrims kept a few sheep, mostly for food, in thatch-roofed sheds near their own simple dwellings. The Pilgrims owned no spinning wheels and their only clothes were the ones they had brought with them from England. But it is possible that they occasionally plucked the fleeces of their sheep to stuff mattresses and pillows.

England banned the export of sheep, but even so, some were smuggled into the American colonies. By 1643, old records show 1,000 of them in Massachusetts. While sheep in early colonial America were kept mainly for meat, soon this would change, and one day, not thousands but millions of sheep would graze the pastures and hillsides of the newest "Promised Land."

3 Custom-Tailored

It is hard to imagine today, when nearly everyone buys clothes "ready to wear" off the racks in stores, that not so long ago every man, woman, and child wore custom-made garments. All clothing was made to order at home, tailored (more or less!) to fit the person who would be wearing it. The rule for most families was:

Use it up, wear it out, make it do or do without!

Many of the warmest, sturdiest, and possibly even the most lastingly beautiful of American homespun textiles were those woolens of medium to darkish colors—browns and grays—and striped fabrics of blue and white or red and white, all colored at home with natural vegetable dyes. The wealthy gentleman or lady tended to wear brighter colors and to have clothing made from imported cottons and silks, but the farmer or laborer was known by his rough, drab homespun, a fabric with a special beauty of its own.

Country men dressed in overblouses or pullovers, known as "frocks," over trousers. Women wore loose dresses and wraparound aprons. Children dressed much like their parents, except that babies and toddlers of both sexes wore dresses. Sometimes people added coats or cloaks, caps, mittens, and stockings. Many people went about their daily chores barefoot, and not only in the summertime.

Colonial folk invented a rough country blend called "linsey-woolsey," a distinctly American textile that combined the warmth of wool with the toughness of linen.

In pastures and meadows close to home, small girls kept an eye on the family sheep, clambering along after the slow-moving flock, higher and higher, and keeping busy all the while with a hand spindle called a "rock," which made a tightly twisted yarn. Of some twenty steps involved in the home manufacture of cloth, most children mastered ten or more.

In colonial America, cloth was indeed manufactured in the home every step of the way. Even after the first textile mills were established in a few New England towns, much cloth was made at home, well past the revolutionary period in rural areas.

Cloth making was traditionally work for women, but men

and boys lent a hand with the heavier tasks, and they were responsible for rounding up the sheep, washing, and shearing them. During the summer, while the menfolk were occupied in the fields, women and girls transformed the raw fleece, step by step, into clothes for the whole family, into bedding and even into twisted skeins of yarn to knit up later.

A fleece was first "scoured"—washed in soap and water and squeezed, to remove lanolin and dirt. In the early days, it was carded entirely by hand, to fluff it and straighten the fibers.

In later colonial times, carding was done at small village mills powered by water from the rushing streams that seemed to be everywhere in New England. Many a farm boy carried fleece that had been carded by hand at home to the village mill on horseback, the fleece carefully done up in an old sheet

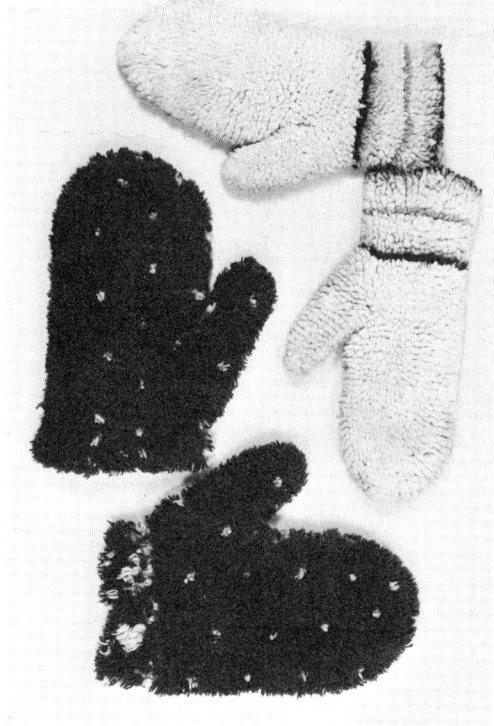

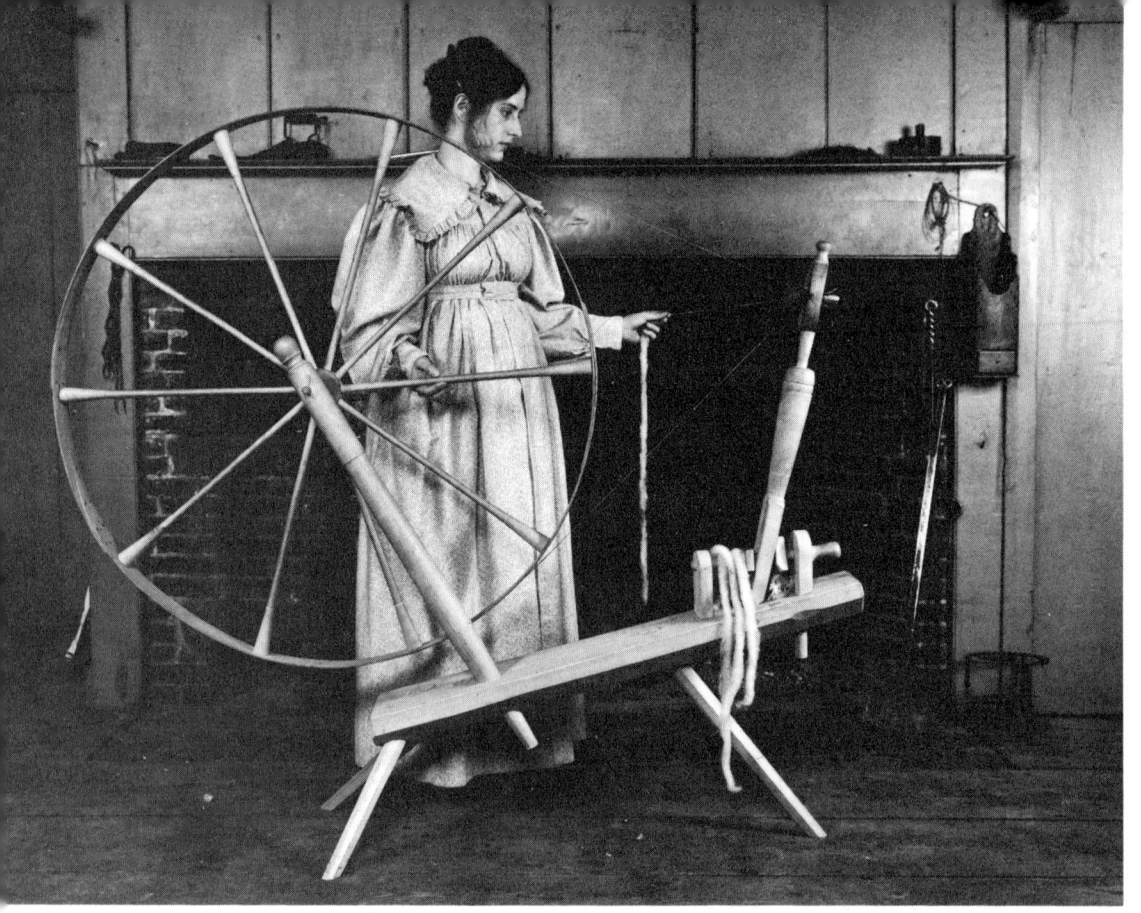

pinned at the four corners with thorns, and the bundle slung over his saddle.

At the mill the fleece was carded a second time by machine, and then carried home again to be spun—once for knitting, twice if it was to be woven.

The wheel for spinning wool was a large, rather fragile-looking wheel beside which the spinner walked back and forth. First, she drew out the carded fibers slowly as she turned the wheel, holding the fibers at just the correct angle to allow them to slip off the point of the revolving spindle and twist into yarn. The spinner stepped backward and paused from time to time to turn the wheel and permit the yarn to wind up on the spindle. She held the yarn slightly taut as the wheel hummed with a kind of moaning, mournful sound. As the strands slipped off the tip of the spindle, she held them high and taut as the wheel quivered and twisted the fibers into yarn. At just the right moment, she glided forward to allow the yarn to slacken slightly and wind.

A spinner could easily walk the equivalent of twenty miles in a day while making the six twisted skeins of yarn considered a good day's work.

The spun yarn was then ready to be dyed. Wool fleece was frequently stripped of some of its natural oils by soaking it in a solution of water and homemade soap (made from saved-up animal fats and from lye that had been leached out of the ashes from household wood fires). But not always! Many seacoast and island dwellers—sailors and fishermen and shore folk in general—preferred to leave wool fleece "as is" to take advantage of its naturally waterproof qualities in rain, snow, sleet, and fog.

Thrifty dyes made from plants made exceptionally soft and lovely hues, and every country household had a wooden dye tub steeping in the corner of the kitchen by the huge open fireplace. With a board on top, the dye tub made a cozy place to sit (if you were careful not to tip it over).

Most people's favorite color was blue; a deep, rich blue could only be achieved from "indigo," a dye purchased from a peddler or at the general store. (Indigo was expensive—it had been imported from the West Indies until the mid-1700s, but was later grown successfully in South Carolina.) In winter, most country men wore the tunics known as "long-shorts," made from blue-and-white striped frocking. Also popular and practical were jackets of "sheep's gray" or of blue-and-white mixed wool, along with heavy blue-and-white socks.

Country people created subtle, naturally beautiful dyes from leaves, berries, bark, and flowers, generally in the range of brown and tan, rose, orange, yellow, dull green, and lavender-gray. Some of the most common were:

    pokeberry juice (deep red)
    dogwood (reddish)
    iris juice (violet)
    onion skins (gold, rust, gray-lavender)
    marigold (orange-brown)
    goldenrod (gold-orange)
    laurel (tan)
    sassafras bark (orange)
    Queen Anne's lace (yellow-tan)
    oak bark, mullein, or peach leaves (yellow)
    black-walnut hulls (warm brown)
    sassafras roots (brown, gray)
    sumac (dull brown)
    butternut bark (gray-green)
    hickory-nut hulls (pinkish beige)
    hickory bark (brown)
    life-everlasting (tan)
    dusty miller (gray)
    lichens (mossy green)
    rhododendron (deep gray-green)
    indigo plus goldenrod (clear green)

Most colonial households owned wool cards and spinning wheels, for both wool and flax. The flax wheel, which was smaller, was sometimes also used to spin shorter wool fibers, whose oily properties helped them stick together. (Cloth made from these short, coarse fibers was rough and tough, but finer flannels and blankets showed a lovely luster from the natural oils in the wool.)

Not all families owned large weaving looms, however, especially in towns where there were professional weavers. In these communities, journeyman-weavers made the rounds from house to house, setting up hand looms in cottage kitchens. Other professional weavers worked at home, accepting yarn on consignment and bringing finished textiles back a few days later.

Weaving is an ancient craft in which cloth is made by interlacing *two* sets of strands *at right angles* to one another. Often, a decorative pattern is created at the time the cloth is made. (Knitting may be an even older craft than weaving. In knitting, the worker interlocks a series of loops by means of one or two needles and a *single* strand of yarn or thread; crocheting is similar to knitting.)

In weaving, the loom is first strung with strong lengthwise strands of linen or cotton, called the "warp." Strands of colored wool, called the "weft" or "woof," are then wound on a shuttle and passed crosswise back and forth over and under the warp strands to create a pattern.

The simplest loom separates every other warp thread to make openings, or "sheds," for the weft. Special devices known as "harnesses" are used to control these separations and create different designs. The more harnesses, the more complicated the designs can be. Early American looms generally had only two or four harnesses, but geometric patterns created on these looms are surprisingly lively and attractive.

4 The Amazing Merino

The early settlers of North America discovered that the garden soil of New England wore out quickly. The terrain was hilly and the soil was incredibly stony, and after a generation or two of intensive farming, crops were poor.

In seventeenth-century America, cash was in short supply, and a man's worth was measured in goods, not money—in furniture, house, barn, tools, and livestock. Various articles served as practical "currencies" of exchange: Indian-style wampum from clam and oyster shells, beaver pelts, tobacco, rice, and wool. Sheep began to play a very important part in the prosperity of the American colonies, particularly in New England. Choice Rhode Island wool became a highly prized form of "money" in local trade.

However, the cows and pigs and sheep that immigrant families brought to America were nothing like the farm animals of today. The runty, scrawny sheep of colonial times were no different from those of medieval Europe. Still, little by little, the people in the colonies, thousands of miles from Europe, began to prosper and then to dare to assert their independence from the "mother country."

For example, in 1661, a few families from Massachusetts moved on to Block Island, a little island some ten miles offshore, and before long their settlement enjoyed a most remark-

31

able good fortune. Gardens bloomed in the sun and salt air, and countless winding paths crisscrossed the moors, paths soon trodden by flocks of sheep grazing free over hill and dale.

By 1680, the little community possessed enough sheep to require that the animals be marked, with each owner's mark registered in the office of the town clerk. These marks were called "earmarks." One quaint old notation read:

> *John Niles his Mark.* A cropp off ye right ear and a hapenny under (ye cropp to be high upon ye eare); a slitt in ye left ear and hapenny under.

Fifteen years later, when sheep still ran at large much of the year, the town fathers began to worry about damage to houses and gardens, and passed a law requiring that sheep be folded, or placed in a common pen, at night. The fine for disobeying was a whopping five pounds!

So it was that on the eve of the War of Independence, the island population consisted of 775 people (whites, blacks, and native Americans)—and more than 2,000 sheep! The Rhode Island Assembly had to order the wartime transfer by boat of nearly all the sheep and lambs to the mainland, to keep the valuable animals from falling into the hands of raiders from the British navy.

Like much of New England, the island's rolling hills and sweet meadows were more than perfect for sheep raising. But while the sheep were large, their wool, as one early observer remarked, was "not the finest." Colonial Americans made do with poor quality wool to replace worn-out bedding and clothing as necessary, but they continued to rely on imported woolens from England. Then, at last, after the Revolution the defiant Yankees found themselves cut off from their old sources of manufactured goods, as well as from familiar markets for American raw materials. Their new political freedom forced them to stand on their own feet and pay their own way in the world.

American leaders, English by heritage, naturally thought of an American woolen industry to compete with the long-established wool industry of Britain. English wool workers and weavers were offered immediate American citizenship on arrival in the New World. Many accepted the offer, and the American wool industry was on its way.

But the wool of common native sheep was barely adequate for home spinning and weaving. What the new United States really needed was a source of the very *best* raw wool. (Presidents Washington and Jefferson chose to wear suits made from American wool at their inaugurations, even though European cloth was far more elegant.)

The first Merino may have arrived in America as early as 1793. Robert Livingston, once chancellor of the state of New York, imported one ram and two ewes for his Hudson Valley manor in 1802. The French immigrant and early industrialist Irénée du Pont brought a Merino ram named Don Pedro to Delaware in 1805, and the ram had become an agricultural celebrity by the time it died in 1811.

George Washington had bred sheep at Mount Vernon, his estate in Virginia, for years, and to improve his own stock he managed to import a number of Merinos from Spain. The Merino bears wool of the finest quality, in great quantity—a purebred Merino may yield 15 to 20 pounds of wool at a single shearing. Merino fleece is dense and very fine, covering the sheep's head and hanging in many loose, heavy folds over its smallish body. With such a splendid wool sheep, America could compete with the best that England had to sell.

The man who really started the Merino craze in America was David Humphreys (1752–1818), a soldier, diplomat, poet, and a friend of Washington. He had served as a secret agent for the American government in Portugal and Spain and become well acquainted with European society, and on his return to America in the early 1800s, he brought a flock of precious Merinos back to his native Connecticut.

Humphreys founded textile mills in the town of Derby, and

DON PEDRO
The Property of E. I. Dupont Esq.

Thomas Jefferson, once a political enemy, became an enthusiastic supporter. By 1810, each of Humphrey's Merinos had a market value of $2,000. There were already some 24 woolen mills operating in the Northeast, manufacturing cloth, rag carpets, and rugs.

The first person to have great numbers of Merinos brought to America was William Jarvis, born in Boston in 1770. Jarvis had a career as a ship's captain and as a merchant and trader in Europe. He served as President Jefferson's consul at Lisbon from 1802 to 1811, running a shipping business of his own at the same time and building a large fortune. In 1808, when the

Emperor Napoleon had conquered Spain and pressed on into Portugal, Jarvis used his money, credit, and personal connections to purchase several thousand selected Merinos and obtained a license to export a shipload of the animals to the United States.

Jarvis had some 4,000 of them distributed throughout the various states along the Eastern Seaboard. Jefferson, who fervently believed in the future of agriculture, invited Jarvis to his home, Monticello, and promised personally to see that Merino flocks were increased in the state of Virginia. Jarvis presented two Merinos apiece to Jefferson and to President James Madison.

Jarvis sold most of his Merinos in New York and Massachusetts, and purchased a farm in Weathersfield, Vermont, on the banks of the Connecticut River. He settled down with 350 Merinos, intending to devote himself to their care and live the life of a country squire in retirement. His flock, according to an eyewitness newspaper report, was

> driven overland to Vermont by a Spanish shepherd, a dark alien-looking man who wore unfamiliar clothes and looked like a picture out of the Old Testament. He looked neither to the right or left as the people of the countryside came to watch, but passed gravely along with eyes only for the fine backs of his flock, which he urged on with unintelligible singing words.

William Jarvis had touched off a wool boom of enormous prosperity in New England—within a few years, 29,000 head of Merinos had been imported; eventually they would multiply into the millions. After Jarvis died, in 1859, his tombstone in the village cemetery at Weathersfield was ornamented with a handsome carved Merino sheep to honor his part in the growth of the American wool industry.

Meanwhile, the fabulous Merino was an American legend and the subject of many a tall tale and rollicking folk song—such as "The Derby Ram," from the Green Mountains of Vermont:

> *As I went down to Derby*
>   *All on a summer's day*
> *'Twas there I saw the biggest sheep*
>   *'Twas ever fed on hay.*
>
> *The horns on this sheep's head, sir,*
>   *They reached up to the moon.*
> *A man went up in February*
>   *And never came down till June.*
>
> *He had four feet to walk, sir,*
>   *He had four feet to stand,*
> *And every foot he had, sir,*
>   *It covered an acre of land.*
>
> *The wool on this sheep's tail, sir,*
>   *I heard the weaver say,*
> *It spun full forty yards, sir,*
>   *And she wove it in a day!*

5 Westward Ho!

In the decades after the Revolution, wool emerged as New England's prize cash crop. Why? Because of a unique combination of circumstances: the nearness of the flocks to the mills where the wool could be processed, along with skilled and hard-working men and women and, not least, abundant waterpower from countless rushing streams.

New Englanders grew their own raw material "by the back door," processed it in cottage and mill, and sold it "out the front door," in the form of far more textiles than they needed for their own personal use. For decades, country housewives had swapped a few pairs of extra mittens at the country stores for factory-made necessities. Now, this old-fashioned bartering, or "'change work," began to grow beyond a simple "cottage industry."

Home-woven cloth tended to be of uneven texture and thin in spots, and for years people had taken it to a certain kind of village mill, called a "fulling mill," for finishing. Fulling was a hand operation, and home weavers brought in cloth for final processing, just as they brought in home-grown corn and rye to a grist mill to be ground into meal and flour, and hand-felled logs to be sawed into boards.

At a fulling mill, cloth was first washed in hot suds and then scoured with "fuller's earth," a kind of absorbent clay. Kept

thoroughly wet all the while in warm soapy water, the cloth was pounded with a large oaken mallet or with rollers. The wool fibers shrank, often by half, as the fabric was allowed to dry in a nearby meadow or stretched on tenterhooks from floor to ceiling in the mill building. At the end of the process, the cloth was smooth and hard.

America's very first woolen textile mill dated from about 1760, and a wool-carding machine of English manufacture had been sold in the United States in the late eighteenth century. Carding by waterpower was first done in 1794, but this did not

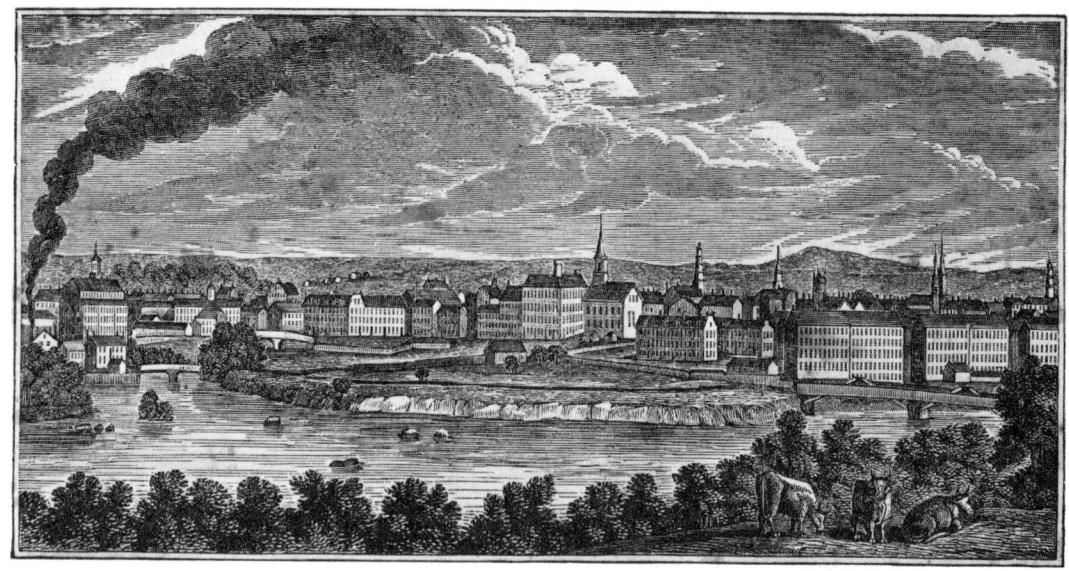

become a common operation for many years. By 1814, however, power looms for weaving were an accepted part of the American factory system. In 1815, Vermont alone had 139 carding mills and 15,000 hand looms busily turning out cloth for a young nation unable to import British goods under President Jefferson's wartime embargo. Vermont remained largely rural, but before long, many fast-growing textile towns in eastern New England were producing miles of cloth. Mill buildings in cities such as Lowell were nothing like the old village mills, with their creaking waterwheels set over clear, tumbling streams. Town factories were massive blocks of brick, with dozens, even hundreds of windows and, often, a handsome clock tower.

There was no more impressive mill complex in all New England than the famous Amoskeag mills on the Merrimack River at Derryfield (now Manchester), New Hampshire. As early as

1793, Samuel Blodgett began building a canal around a "hideous waterfall," and fourteen years later he finished it. Still keen when he was in his eighties, Blodgett proclaimed grandly, "As the country increases in population we must have manufactures, and here, at my canal, will be a manufacturing town that shall be the Manchester of America." He was referring to England's great (and gloomy) industrial city, and his prophecy, for better or worse, came true.

The great brick pavilions on both sides of the river took advantage of a vast source of waterpower, plenty of money from rich investors in Boston, and of course the finest raw wool from the Merinos of the northern hill country. It was an unbeatable combination!

Soon cotton was added, grown in the rich black earth of the South and brought to New England in Yankee-owned ships, woven in Yankee mill towns, and returned to the South as finished piece goods. It did not seem to matter to many people at that time that Yankee children performed much of the labor in the mills for pennies, and that most of the fabric was intended to be used for cheap work clothes for slaves.

By 1831, the Amoskeag Cotton and Wool Manufactory had become the Amoskeag Manufacturing Company. It owned all the waterpower between Concord and Manchester and all of the land at the great sixty-foot falls. A stone dam had replaced the original wooden one, and the canals behind the dam brought water to the waterwheels of an astonishing complex of factories that eventually branched out into manufacturing paper, tools, fire engines, and even locomotives for the thrilling "iron horse"

—the railroad network that was revolutionizing transportation and opening up the West.

Up-country, the hillsides were swarming with sheep. By 1840, there were more than 2¼ million sheep in New Hampshire and Vermont alone, two-thirds of these in the valleys of the Green Mountains and along the shores of Lake Champlain. Vermont had five times as many sheep as people.

"Merino money" built splendid mansions to replace many of the simpler homesteads of the past. So bright was the future of sheep raising that one Vermont farmer could afford to *turn down* an offer of $10,000 for his best ram. Another farmer, people whispered, refused $50,000—a fortune in those days—for his flock of 200 ewes.

As the colonial "cottage industry" became big business, the quality of life changed. A few families prospered, but for many people, life was not what it had been. The mills were dismal and cold in the winter, stifling hot in summer. Children spent six days a week in the mills replacing bobbins of thread instead of tending lambs, fishing, berry picking, and helping out in the garden.

Many people left home to work long hours in the mills. They used their cash wages for store-bought goods, since they had no more time to grow all their food and make things by hand.

Others left their small hill farms behind and headed for the fertile plains of the West. Once more, sheep went along! In the mid-nineteenth century, eastern wool sheep mingled with the millions of mutton sheep that had long roamed the prairies. So began the modern American sheep industry, with sheep raised today for both meat and wool.

As the source of supply for raw wool shifted westward to Colorado, Nebraska, Texas and other states, the New England wool industry was doomed to failure. Giant brick mill complexes were gradually abandoned or converted to other uses. Many of them are still standing—looms and bobbins quiet, windowpanes smashed, bricks crumbling and faded. Many an old village mill, too, is a tumbledown ghost, with a mossy waterwheel half rotted beside a murky pond clogged with grasses.

Yet fortunately, there are people who care about the old ways, the old-fashioned methods that lovingly and painstakingly created everyday necessities of such beauty. Landmarks-preservation groups are rescuing old mills, for nowadays, people know that a humble village mill or a dingy brick factory can be just as fascinating as a palace.

Here and there, these buildings are being transformed into design centers, shops, and mini-museums, and dedicated craftspeople everywhere are reviving a part of our colorful past that was not so "long ago" at all! Wool is fun to work with—why not see for yourself!

How to Design and Knit a Quick Muffler

For an old-fashioned "country" style, choose one of the all-wool yarns known as Icelandic or Irish-fisherman types. These come in natural undyed shades of creamy white, tan, gray, brown, and black—some colors are quite solid, others are flecked or mixed in appearance. These yarns are naturally water-repellent and bulky but light in weight. They are not very tightly twisted, so be careful not to yank or tug them, or the fibers may separate and the strand may break.

You can buy a skein or two of yarn for your muffler, of course, but if you know someone who knits a lot, you can make a unique muffler by using leftover yarns. Create your own pattern of stripes by changing colors and by working with assorted scraps. You can mix different kinds of yarn as you wish, as long as you use only those yarns that are fairly similar in weight and thickness. Use your imagination and save money!

With bulky yarns, use large knitting needles—size 11 or 13 would be good. Fat needles make huge stitches and a muffler with a loose, open pattern of loops and holes that will feel very warm wrapped around your neck in cold and blustery weather! Your project will go fast, because it takes just three or four stitches or rows to measure one inch of muffler.

Cast on about 20 stitches—more if you want a wider scarf—and knit each row back and forth until your scarf is as long as you want. (This is called "garter stitch" and makes a ridged "crunchy" fabric.) Then, bind off.

To add a fringe, clip pieces of yarn about 8 inches long, fold several in half to make a loop, and draw the loop through a corner of the muffler end, using a large crochet hook to guide it. Slip the yarn ends through the loop and *gently* pull taut to make a knot. Continue in this manner across both ends of your muffler, always keeping the same side of the scarf facing you as you go, until your fringe is completed.

Index

Africa, North, 16, 20–21
alpaca, 14
Amoskeag factory, 40
Arabs, 21

Babylon, 20
bighorn, 14
Block Island, R.I., 31–33
Blodgett, Samuel, 41

carding, 13, 25–26, 29; see also mills
clothing, 13, 20, 22–25, 28, 33
commons, 10–11, 32
Connecticut, 8, 34
crocheting, 20, 30

"Derby Ram, The," 37
Don Pedro, 34–35
du Pont, Irénée, 34
dyeing, 23, 27–28

England, 21, 33

flax, 13, 29
"fuller's earth," 38

Greece, 20
Green Mountains, 37, 42

hair, 14–15, 18; see also wool
Hebrews, 21
Humphreys, David, 34–35
Jarvis, William, 35–37
Jefferson, Thomas, 34–36, 40

keratin, 14
knitting, 20, 22, 26, 30
"linsey-woolsey," 24
"Little Gray Lady by the Sea," see Nantucket
Livingston, Robert, 34
looms, 29–30, 40
Lowell, Mass., 40

Madison, James, 36
Manchester, N.H., 40–41
Massachusetts, 10–12, 22, 31, 36, 40
Merino, 18, 21, 34–37, 41–42
mills: carding, 26, 39–40; fulling, 38–39; grist, 38–39; textile, 24–25, 35, 39–41, 44
Monticello, 36
moufflon, 18–19

Nantucket, Mass., 10–13
Near East, 16, 20–21
New Hampshire, 40–42

Pilgrims, 22
ponds, 8–9, 11–12
Portugal, 34–36

Quakers, 10–12

railroads, 41–42
Revolution, American, 33, 38
Rhode Island, 31–33
Robinson, Rowland, 7
"rock," 24

Rocky Mountains, 18–19
Romans, 21
"rueing," 15–16; see also shearing

scouring, 25
shearing, 7–12, 25; see also "rueing"
sheep: breeds of, 18–19; care of, 8, 11; domestication of, 14, 18–20; habits of, 11, 18–19; raising of, in American West, 44
shepherds, 11, 19, 36
Spain, 21, 34, 36
spinning, 12–13, 22, 24, 26–27, 29, 33; see also mills

textiles, 13, 20–21, 23, 24, 29, 33, 38–40, 44

Vermont, 7, 36–37, 40, 42

Washington, George, 34
water power, 38–41
Weathersfield, Vt., 36–37
weaving, 29–31, 33; see also mills
Winchester, England, 21
wool: properties of, 14–18, 27, 29, 34; trade in, 20–21, 31; see also hair

47

About the Author

Elizabeth Gemming is a New Englander at heart. A descendant of *Mayflower* pilgrims, she was born on Long Island, spent many summers in southern New Hampshire as a child, and was graduated from Wellesley College in Massachusetts. Among the twelve books she has written are *Born in a Barn*, *Maple Harvest*, and *Lost City in the Clouds: The Discovery of Machu Picchu*.

Mrs. Gemming lives in New Haven, Connecticut. Her husband, Klaus, is a book designer. They have two children, Marianne and Christina. Mrs. Gemming's hobbies include knitting, which she was taught (by an aunt) at the age of seven and a half!

j636.3
Gemming, E
   Wool gathering

MRL

NOV 2 2 2013

State of Vermont
Department of Libraries
Midstate Regional Library
RFD #4
Montpelier, Vt. 05602

DATE DUE